Happy cooky baking
Gwen Welk W.

My Cooky Journal
Sharing Life's Lessons and a Cooky

Gwen Welk Workman

© Gwen Workman, 2021.

ISBN No. 978-0-9717377-1-6

Printed and bound in the United States of America. All rights reserved. No part of this book may be reproduced or transmitted in any form or by any means, electronically or mechanically, including photocopying, recording, or by an information storage and retrieval system, except by a reviewer who may quote brief passages in a review to be printed in a magazine or newspaper—without permission in writing from the publisher. For information, please contact Wooden Spoon Press, 1617 K Avenue, Plano, TX 75074.

Dedication

To everyone whose lives touched mine through my cookies. To my mother, Estelle Lien Welk, who taught me patience, quality, and beauty so that my cookies become not just food, but works of art. To my family and friends, for encouraging me by eating and critiquing my cookie masterpieces. To Virginia Jonas Lawrence for helping me with my first edition of "A Cooky Journal." She has been a help and a true inspiration.

Sprinkle some great cookie crumbs in your journey through life. Enjoy the simple pleasures.

My Cooky Journey

It is often said that a kitchen is the heart of the home. It symbolizes food, which symbolizes security, health, and happiness. Food is attached to a range of emotions. Health food is associated with nourishment, hot food is associated with comfort, and dessert food is associated with celebration and joy. Cookies are a common and universal food. Each cookie harnesses the comfort of a hot bowl of soup and the fun of a birthday party.

I would like to take you on a cooky journey and share with you the many wonderful opportunities cookies have given me to spread joy and lift the spirits of the people I have met along the way.

Scandinavians love cookies! My mother was Norwegian: a wonderful cook, and teacher.

Under her instruction, I learned to make different variations of Scandinavian cookies such as Sunbakkels, Fattigmann, Date-filled, Berlin-A-Kranse, Sugar, Spritz, Pepperkaker, Hermits, and Krumkaker. It is common for a Scandinavian hostess to serve seven kinds of cookies to her guests during the Christmas holiday, so true to my heritage, I learned how to prepare a variety of cookies to serve to guests or give as gifts.

My desire to bake began early, as a young girl just past ten. My mother's love of baking sparked my interest as I watched her. Somehow, blending flour, sugar, butter, and eggs to create something so scrumptious intrigued me. Each recipe provided instructions and ingredients that, when combined, resulted in delicious little cookies.

I started my baking career by following the directions of each cookie recipe exactly as it was written. This taught me to analyze the recipes for fat content, flavor, blending of flavors, and ratios of liquids to solids. I quickly determined which ones would become the most flavorful, the most delicate, and the prettiest cookies, simply by reading the list of ingredients. I discovered combinations and various manipulations to create the most delectable cookies possible.

This determination and skill combined with the love of creating led me to develop new cookies and recipes. To ensure that the cookies remained the same, I converted the cups to pounds. Using a scale allows a baker to replicate the recipe exactly if the scale measures both pounds and ounces. This device is an invaluable investment for all types of baking. Remember: You can heap a cup, but you cannot heap a pound!

My family was large, and each member was responsible for the other. My brothers went to work with my father while the girls helped Mother with housework. When I was a teenager, I had a summer job as a waitress. The hours were long, and the work was hard, but fulfilling. My sister Marilyn, my friend Arlene and I worked in town during the week. I worked in a family restaurant owned by a Swedish couple and Marilyn and Arlene worked in a gift shop. I served meals, scrubbed floors, and did odd jobs. At night, we slept in the "Doll

House." It was our own little house, and we took much pride in maintaining it. The downstairs held a little kitchen, living room, and dining room. The upstairs held our three beds. Since town was twelve miles from home and we did not have transportation, we lived in the "Doll House" during the week and went to our family homes on our days off. I eagerly anticipated the weekend, as I wanted to see my younger siblings.

Cookies were always a welcomed treasure. I knew how excited the children

became when they were baked, and the containers were full. When the family had gone for the day to do the chores, I entertained my two-year old twin brothers while baking cookies. Some of the money from my week's wages went toward the ingredients I experimented with. I baked spiced cookies, coconut cookies topped with cherries, icebox cookies and "rocks," which were spiced cookies with raisins. That was my choice and I loved creating a new cookie. My mother owned several wooden boxes with glass covers from her parents' stores. Each box was filled to the brim with various treats. I would spend the entire day measuring, mixing, blending, forming, and baking, simply to watch the cookies disappear into waiting, hungry mouths. My reward was to watch the pleasure of my younger siblings as they enjoyed them.

For my wedding, I had decided that I did not want a wedding reception where people sat and ate, but one where people mingled and conversed. With

this in mind, I decided to serve small delicate cookies and finger sandwiches. With the help of my sister Marilyn, and the attendants, Joan and Arlene, we made all the cookies and open-faced sandwiches to serve to our guests.

We spent days preparing the miniature masterpieces. Tiny ribbon and checkerboard sandwiches were created from light and dark breads. Little

round cookie-cutter sandwiches were iced with cheese spread. The bakery prepared blue-tinted loaves of bread which added to the festivity. The cookie selection consisted of tiny spritz cookies, butter cookies, Russian tea cookies, gingersnaps, chocolate chip and raisin-filled cookies. Each was as light as air and melted on the tongue. Since then, cookies have played an important role in countless celebrations for my new family.

Typically, people are the most generous during the Christmas season, and I followed my mother's tradition of baking the seven kinds of cookies for the holidays. However, I wondered why this spirit does not seem to exist throughout the remainder of the year. Charities and individuals in need receive the bulk of their contributions during Christmas and but not during the rest of the year. Why should we enjoy this wonderful array of cookies only at Christmas?

I solved the problem by spending a day baking several varieties of cookies. I arranged them in containers to freeze. Now my freezer always looked like a celebration! When guests arrived, I would take out an assortment. By that time, the coffee was percolated, and the cookies were thawed and ready to serve.

With this kind of year-round sharing in mind, I decided to focus my efforts not at Christmas, but at an unexpected time. I chose Valentine's Day as a time to celebrate with the community elders and lighten their spirits with a cookie. I discovered a way to not only donate to seniors, but to spend time with my children as well. When my children, Jim, Stuart, and Shelly, were small, between the ages of three and eight, they would invite friends over to help bake cookies. Sherrie, Kim, Jamie, and Joe often served as aides. The seven children would squeeze around the small kitchen table, so each could have a hand in the dough. Each child rolled dough, used the cookie cutters, and decorated the individual masterpieces. When the cookies were done baking, the kids arranged them on trays for delivery. They all took such great pride in their work and handled the tiny cookies as though they were delicate works of art, which amused and delighted the elderly people. Eight-year-old Jamie wrote an article for the school paper describing our Valentine's Day tradition. He stated, "We have been doing this for years."

After I began the tradition of distributing cookies, I could not have stopped without disappointing the elderly and losing precious time with my rapidly growing children. As a den leader for Cub Scouts, I found a way to continue baking Valentine's Day cookies – I had to slightly altar my methods. Since the troop was too large to huddle around the kitchen table, I had to alter my methods slightly. By preparing the dough the night before, time was not wasted during the meeting, and the boys could spend all their time cutting and decorating the cookies. After waiting for the cookies to bake, which seemed to be much too long for hungry young boys, each child was able to eat his fill. Afterwards, the boys took the plentiful leftovers to the seniors' homes and handed them out. They were delighted with the cookies and the time spent with the children. Although the boys could have done this deed and accepted the cookies as their reward, community service badges provided an added incentive.

Enjoyable times with countless people have come through my cookie distribution. One of the most touching and prominent memories involves an elderly man named Roy Rose. Roy had lived down the road from my family since I was a small girl. He was tall, unkempt, and not completely shaven. He always wore a flannel shirt and khaki pants, held up by suspenders. He was well into his eighties and in need of some support. He became one of the Valentine's Day cookie recipients. I went to his house with a beautiful package of cookies, wrapped in a bow. When he opened the door, it became evident that he had never mastered the art of cleaning. Smells of kerosene and tobacco came pouring out. Despite all the clutter, or possibly because of it, he was thrilled with the pretty package. As a gesture of gratitude, he leaned over and placed a careful and tender kiss on my cheek. To this day, I remember that moment. My action was so simple and yet he was genuinely grateful for the little bit of friendship that I had extended to him.

At one time I owned a restaurant, so it became necessary to convert the cookie recipes to commercial size to keep up with demand. My practice of using weight rather than volume measurement was the key to preserving the quality of the cookies. First, the ingredients were weighed, and then the dough. Maintaining this process ensured that every cookie was identical to the next, and customers were guaranteed a consistent product. After investing so much time and energy into developing the perfection of each soft, chewy cookie, I was dismayed by one man's request.

Bill, the city maintenance man, was a regular at the restaurant. Every morning at 10 am, he arrived and ordered a cup of coffee and a cookie. I was absolutely astonished the day he ordered a "hammer" cookie. I had never received a single complaint about hard cookies and despised the thought that after all these years, my efforts had not been successful. I decided that I would ask for an explanation before I became overly distraught. The next days he came in, sat down, and ordered a "hammer" cookie. I brought the coffee to him with the large sugar cookie on a little saucer. I then asked why he had given that title to my cookie. He then raised his fist into the air and dropped it onto the cookie, as though his hand were a "hammer." This action caused the cookie to break into several bite size pieces, perfect for eating with coffee. I was relieved to learn that my cookies were not called "hammer" because they were hard, but because they were not bite size!

After the children had grown up and started their careers, Jim and I decided to move to Texas. Afterwards, I learned that Bill had suffered a stroke. I spent some time reminiscing about the past, "hammer" cookies and the admiration that my eldest son, Jimmy, had for him. He had called him "Mr. Bill Condon," and was in absolute awe of the machines he drove. I guess driving a tractor is an impressive skill to a six-year-old boy.

To let "Mr. Bill Condon" know that he was in my prayers, I wanted to send a gift. I went to the store and purchased a small plastic hammer. I then filled a tin with sugar cookies and attached it to the top with tape. You can imagine his surprise after receiving a package of cookies from Texas.

I spent many long hours running the restaurant, so I was not able to devote much time as a volunteer for charitable organizations, but I always searched for missions I could do while working. I would like to share two examples:

Dr. Mullihan had spent many years as a family physician. He and his wife Margaret moved to our community after his retirement. Even then, he continued to share his talents, but a stroke confined him to his home. Margaret would occasionally come into the restaurant for a meal. Most of the time I was able to sit down with her for a few minutes to visit, and we would talk about the events of the week. It was not easy for her to care for her beloved husband while working full time. She shared with me how much he loved sweets. The end of each visit would find her walking out the door with a special treat for "Doc" from me. His favorite was a gingersnap cookie or a cream pie. On Margaret's next visit she told me how much he enjoyed his treat.

I had known Harold Forbes since I was a teenager and babysat next door to his house. He was a tall, stout man, who stooped over when he walked. Each Sunday, he came to the restaurant to visit his friends. He was in his seventies, yet he continued to work as a mechanic. Despite his greasy job, his wife, Nan, never failed to keep him clean and tidy. She had smoked cigarettes for years and suffered from emphysema. She carried an oxygen tank with her, making it nearly impossible to leave the house. She was, however, able to maintain it and do the laundry. Harold treated himself to a pancake with his friends once a week, but he did not want to deny Nan a treat, even though she could not come to the restaurant with him. Each week, I would place a glazed donut in a white sack and ask him to take it home for her. She became so excited when he walked into the house carrying the little sack. I received the most beautiful thank-you notes and words of love. Accompanying one of them was a beautiful lucky feather. The Chippewa Indians believe giving the gift of an lucky feather would bring good luck to the recipient. I was deeply grateful for Nan and Harold's desire to share good fortune with others, in the face of her illness.

I would ask myself often, "What did I really give away?" I have discovered that what I give to others is returned to me in a gift of greater value. To share the real things in life was a lesson my mother instilled in my siblings and I. At a rather young age, she taught us that we must practice the art of the

mustard seed by sowing tiny seeds of love and kindness.

Each day, try to bring joy, a smile, or a laugh to someone. For me, this is easily done by serving or giving away a cookie. It is not only the cookie someone receives, but an act of kindness and fellowship. Share your day, sprinkle someone with a few cookie crumbs, and see how great your day can be!

In January of 1985, Plano, Texas, became my new home. Upon arrival, I discovered that it was quite different from our home in Longville, Minnesota. I suffered from a bit of culture shock. I felt as though I was in a completely new land. Every aspect of life seemed to differ from what I had known. The heat was unbearable, the ground was dry and hard and even the bugs were unfamiliar. The ones in Minnesota flew; here they crawled. In Longville, they were soft; here they crunched loudly underneath careless feet. I had lost the sense of community and friendship that accompanied small-town

life. I was surrounded by strangers in the stores, where I would have known everyone by name in Longville. I desperately needed to make friends.

I began using cookies as an icebreaker. I took them to my neighbors and church groups. I filled my days with baking. After an adjustment period, I realized my strong desire to create a place where individuals like myself could feel comfortable.

Shortly after moving to Allen, my reputation as a cookie baker was well established. We had not lived in our new house very long when the neighborhood children began to visit. It was common for them to simply knock on the door and want to come in to visit. The kids and I talked about school while they ate cookies.

One night, as I returned home, three boys appeared. I was familiar with them, as they had enjoyed countless cookies with me. They saw the bags of groceries and asked, "Can we carry your groceries for you, Mrs. Workman?"

I had never asked, or expected anything from them, but I thought this was a good exchange for a few cookies. I was glad to make a connection with the kids and liked the fact that they enjoyed helping me. For several years, until they became teenagers, I never carried in my groceries.

One night, about seven o'clock, I decided to make sugar cookies. I was spending the time alone, and my thoughts ran rampant. I thought of my friend Josh. He had diligently carried my groceries into the house for years and was now a nice young man. About four years earlier, he lost his mother suddenly. I felt sad for him because he no longer had anyone to bake cookies for him. I decided to call him and invite him over. I wanted company and knew how much Josh had always loved the cookies.

When I called, his father informed me that he was at work and would not be home until 9:30 pm. He worked at a skating rink in Dallas and at 10 pm, I heard a knock on the front door. I was pleasantly surprised to see Josh standing on the porch. It had been quite a while since I last saw him. Now, at sixteen, he was so good-looking and so adult, but he still held a childlike affection for cookies. A couple of years later when he graduated from Allen High School, I sent him a card. This is the thank-you note I received in return.

Dear Gwen,

Thank you for the card. I am very glad that ya'll are thinking about me. I need to get a bunch of cookies before I go off to college!

Love,

Josh

In September of 1988, I opened The Wooden Spoon: a Scandinavian shop in McKinney, Texas. I filled it with items that were reminiscent of my home and Scandinavian heritage. Drawing from my experiences in the restaurant, I started catering parties, baking, and cooking. I began to remember my customers' names and faces and regained a sense of community.

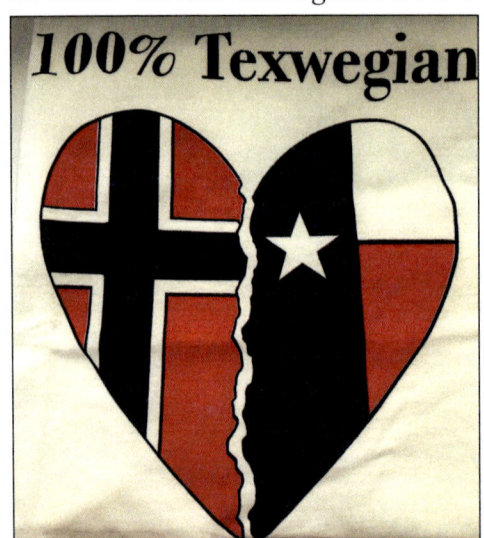

It did not take long before I was recognized for my cookies, just like in Longville. Through this course of events, I reconciled with my new Texas home and my "Texwegian" status.

The love of cookies does not have an expiration date.

One of my customers at The Wooden Spoon, Barbara, began to bring her mother to shop with her. Over time, I became closer to them and learned more about their family. Barbara's mother had moved from Chicago to be with her daughter when she was diagnosed with cancer. One day, as they browsed, Barbara's mother said, "You can't get a good cup of soup here in Plano." I thought about what she said and realized that she was right.

That night at home, my thought turned to her and another man, Carl, who suffered from cancer. He also loved soup and could no longer eat much else. I decided to make a pot of chicken noodle soup. As it cooked, I decided that soup alone would not suffice. I also prepared homemade bread and cookies.

That night, I delivered the meals to them. After all these years, the families of these two beautiful people remember the meal. They were astonished that people who did not know them well would take the time to do such a kind thing.

However, my sensibilities were developed through years of my life in a small town where everybody took care of each other. My thought was, "How many requests can be fulfilled for somebody with cancer? There is so little time left for them, and her request was small and easy to fulfill."

In 1989, a friend of mine mentioned a pre-school for children meeting each day at Resurrection Lutheran in Plano. It was open to families from various walks of life, and tuition was on a sliding scale, based on need. To keep it functioning, donations were sought. I wanted to contribute but wanted to share something more personal than money, so I volunteered to bring cookies once a month.

Interestingly, the language of cookies is spoken by all socio-economic brackets. The children inevitably loved each cookie, from sugar to ginger. After donating for over a year, I was pleased when the children visited Fairview Farms for a tour, where my shop was located. When they arrived in my shop the teacher said, "Class, this is Mrs. Workman. Can you say good morning? This is the lady with the big cookies." After an overwhelming greeting from the exuberant children, we all shared a cookie.

When Jim and I moved to Texas, he joined the Lions Club, to become involved with the community. After some time, he eventually became president of his chapter. However, as time passed and his company began to pick up an increasing amount of work, he was forced to drop his membership.

One day, while we were shopping, we recognized two men from the club. After saying hello, Jim said, "Do you remember my wife?"

They replied instantly. "Yes, and we remember she makes the best cookies."

I may not have been close to them, but at least they knew of my cookies.

I was absolutely amazed by this comment. Even though we had attended many meetings over a two-year period, the cookies stood out more prominently in their minds than we did. Are you sprinkling cookie crumbs yet?

My signature at The Wooden Spoon always has been to have the coffee percolated and cookies available. When we offer coffee to customers, we say, "If you need cream, sugar, or a cookie, you will find them on the counter." A cookie is usually the first choice.

Cookies, as I discovered, are also required when learning. At the store, classes in Scandinavian languages and arts are offered. Classes are held for two hours, and it is necessary to maintain concentration. It has become my trademark to serve a cup of coffee and a cookie to every student. Each class day, when I open the shop, first thing in the morning, I perk the coffee and set out a tray of cookies. The students have commented, "We really look forward to the cookies." If the cookie tray is not present, when the students arrive for class, they promptly bring the error to my attention so I can remedy the situation.

My eldest grandson, Brandon, has been a strong supporter of my gingersnaps since he was young. He never failed to request a gingersnap and preferred them over any of the others. One day, he came to the store and to help me package and put prices on the sugar, gingersnaps, lemon-iced, and oatmeal cookies.

He asked, "Grandma, how much is each cookie?" When I told him and he learned the gingersnap was one of the least expensive, he strongly disagreed with me. "Grandma," he said, "the gingersnaps should be the most expensive because they are the best."

I met a young lady, Diana, at church one Sunday. She expressed interest in making lefse and I encouraged her to learn to prepare it. Her husband decided he would like to take it up too. She came into the store to purchase the necessary items with her eight-month-old son. After we exchanged pleasantries and had a short conversation, I turned my attention to her son. He was an adorable little boy, and I decided to share a cookie with him. I picked up a lemon-iced sugar cookie, broke it in half, and offered it to him. His happy expression became downtrodden, and he buried his face in his mother's neck. I felt as though I must be the stingiest person in the world. How selfish to only offer half a cookie! I put the broken one down and picked up a fresh, unspoiled cookie. His renewed happiness was evident, and he enjoyed his cookie.

In 1992, I purchased the oldest home in Plano to move the Wooden Spoon to its permanent location. It is quite spacious, so it not only provides an area to sell the gifts and food from Scandinavia, but also a place for teaching and hosting parties and meetings.

Magnus was a gorgeous little Norwegian boy. His mother began shopping in the store when it was located at Fairview Farms. He was only six years old at the time but still knew how many of each item to pick up, and he would arrange his purchase neatly beside the register. He was always cheerful and a delightful visitor. I grew closer to him through the years. His mother taught Norwegian classes at the store, so I saw him quite often. Each time he came into the store, we traded hugs for cookies. It was standard protocol to say hello, hug, and eat a cookie. The family moved back to Norway, but I still believe that even though he was enjoying the cookies, the hugs were far sweeter.

The Swedish school meets upstairs each Wednesday. While some of the students were shy and did not visit with me, one young boy, Robin, had no qualms about becoming my friend. Before he went to class, he would come in the shop, look around at the merchandise, make comments, grab a gingersnap, and run up the stairs to class. One day, I said, "Please come here." He came over and looked up at me, slightly timidly. I said, "If you are going to eat my cookies, the least I should get is a hug." A smile slowly spread across his face and he threw his arms around my neck. Now he comes in, immediately gives me a big hug, takes a cookie, and goes to class. I was not accustomed to visiting with him after class, so I was rather surprised one day. We had already run through the ritual, but he came into the shop after class. He came up to me, looked up, and said, "I don't need a cookie, I just need a hug." Sometimes the comfort found in a cookie can also be found in the person who provides it.

John, a close friend, was responsible for lawn maintenance in the Allen School District. I had been in McKinney on business and drove past the yard workers on the way back to my house. They were mowing and trimming at a neighborhood elementary school and looked rather hot out in the sun. After I returned home and changed my clothes, I was ready to return to the Wooden Spoon, when I thought of John. I wrapped two sugar cookies in plastic wrap

and pulled a cold can of soda out of the refrigerator. On my way back to the store, I stopped by the school. John was elated to receive the cookies and soda. He was so proud to be given a surprise. He has retold the story countless times. He was so thankful, not only for the treat but for the small amount of individual attention that made him feel special.

I was reminiscing about my Aunt Muriel, remembering all the kindness she had shown me. I decided to send a dozen gingersnaps to her because they were her favorite. A week later, I received a telephone call from her. She was so happy to share a cookie story with me. A few of her childhood friends had come over for a visit. She served my cookies along with a pot of coffee and as they ate and chatted about recent developments, one of the men abruptly changed the subject.

"I haven't had cookies like this since I ate them at Grandma's," he exclaimed.

The flavor had stirred a vivid memory in his mind, and he was so thrilled. When I hung up the telephone, I felt so proud to have made him happy. I like possessing the ability to bring contentment through something as simple as a cookie. Who would have guessed that my gingersnaps would bring back wonderful memories of his grandma?

In March of 1997, I flew to Minneapolis to attend a buyers' show. I like to attend the show for two reasons. First, I like meeting and visiting with people who share my fascination with Scandinavian culture. Secondly, I love having an excuse to go to Minnesota and spend time with four of my grandsons and their parents.

On this trip, I rented a car and needed to compact my luggage as much as possible. I knew that I would disappoint the boys unless I brought treats for them, but I also needed room to pack my clothes and other essentials. After much contemplation, I settled on a medium-sized suitcase. I managed to squeeze in four dozen cookies and three packages of Daim® Swedish candies. When I arrived at my son Stu and daughter-in-law Jackie's home, I unpacked the goodies. Their two sons, Evan and Nick were delighted and quickly claimed them.

On Wednesday, I needed to leave for my daughter Shelly and son-in-law Andrew's home. I thought of Benjamin and Sam's elation upon receiving the candy and cookies and could not bring myself to ask for the return of the remaining cookies and candy. I spent my time in the car struggling to think of something to give to my other grandsons, Benjamin and Sam. When I arrived at their home, Benjamin came running down the stairs calling: "Grandma, Grandma!" He threw his little arms around me, tucked his feet at my waist, and said, "Did you bring me any cookies?"

My heart sank. "No, Benjamin," I said, "Grandma didn't, but we're going to make bread."

The next day, we got the yeast and flour and made the most wonderful rolls. Benjamin loved the them, but it was the raw dough he could not get enough of. The homemade rolls turned out to be a good substitute for the missing cookies. The rolls were not the cookies that they were so accustomed to, but I think they loved them because we made them together.

Right before the annual St. Lucia pageant, a couple with a five-year-old boy came into the shop. I served coffee and cookies as they shopped. The father was American, and the mother was Swedish. As a result, the child was bilingual. At his young age, he had already figured out which language to speak to which parent. I asked him if he was in the pageant. His father overheard what I had asked and said, "Sing her the pepperkaker song."

He became visibly shy and embarrassed and asked his father,

"Dad, why do you always make me do this?"

After much coaxing, he sang the song in Swedish to me. He was adorable and I was amazed by his ability.

In August, he returned to visit the shop with his parents. Immediately upon arrival, he went directly to the cookie tin, took out one cookie, and asked his mother if he could have it. His mother became embarrassed by his forward attitude, but I consoled her. I told her that children remember where the cookies and the toys are.

I first met Tommi approximately thirty years ago. I was struggling to expand my business, and she worked for a local loan agency. Throughout the course of a few years, when working closely on my business transactions, Tommi became more of a friend than an acquaintance. When I invited her to a party that I was hosting, I met her husband Tracy for the first time. I enjoy making friends and meeting new people and Tracy made this very easy.

I take great pride in my cooking. Any compliment in that department will take the compliment giver a long way. After finishing dinner, Tracy said, "I would like to meet whoever made that meal so I can kiss her hands." I held out my hands to him and he placed a kiss on each one. From then on, Tracy kissed my hands whenever he eats my cooking. As sweet as this action is, it cannot go without reciprocation. Tracy is the cook of his household, so naturally I would kiss his hands when he was the chef. Not long after I became friends with Tracy he discovered my lemon-iced cookies. They are his favorite, even though he does eat them in a strange way.

When he comes to visit, I turn my back to him as he steals a cookie from the tray. He claims that the cookies taste better because they have more value when stolen. Ever since he began stealing my cookies, he has not been able to break the habit and can no longer eat an offered cookie. This behavior is not just for my amusement either, as I had thought before. Tracy and Tommi were remodeling, and I thought I would be nice and send a few cookies to them, but Tracy requested that the cookie bag be placed on the counter so that he could steal one when nobody was looking. After he stole his cookie, he shared the rest with the painters. Everybody agreed they tasted delicious.

After years of cookie theft, Tracy finally became upset with me.

The Christmas season is the busiest time of year in the store and I was overwhelmed with work. I realized that I did not have enough time to make cookies and lefse, so I had to eliminate the cookies. When Tracy heard that I was not making cookies, he felt the need to share his distress.

We were at a dinner party with our friends and Tracy brought up the cookie shortage repeatedly. After several failed attempts to find sympathy, he announced that he was not going to visit again until January 15th. He said that I would have time to recover from the holiday season and bake if he waited that long. By the time the 15th came, I had prepared a special tray of cookies to be stolen.

Unfortunately, fate did not allow Tracy's crimes to go unpunished. Once Tracy was firmly in the habit of stealing cookies, he suffered a heart attack. I felt terrible and missed visiting with my friend. I asked to see if I could do anything to help, and I received a message from him. Tracy claimed that the attack was brought on by all the cream of tartar in the lemon-iced cookies. When he returned home, he said, "Tartar appears on your teeth, but cream of tartar clogs your arteries."

One night, my grandson, Benjamin called me. He updated me on all the recent occurrences in his life. We had been talking for a while when he said, "Grandma, Brenda (his babysitter) and I made cookies, but they didn't turn out. Do you think you could send us some?"

I once offered a cookie to a young Swedish boy, whose mother had been a customer for a while. I pointed him in the direction of the cookie tin. It is always in the same place. He walked over and helped himself to one, looked up at me, and said, "My little brother would like one, but he's in the car."

His mother and I laughed. I could not deprive a child of a cookie, so I gave the boy another for his brother, while his mother continued to shop. After about fifteen minutes passed, they were ready to purchase their items and leave when I noticed that his brother's cookie had vanished. I decided to do a little detective work. I asked him where the other cookie was, and he hung his head. I did not want him to feel sad over something as silly as a cookie, so I said, "those cookies are so good you can't eat only one, right?"

Of course, he agreed with me and appeared relieved.

I said, "Come on and we'll get another one for your brother." Then they left, and his little brother received the much-anticipated cookie.

Now that companies are more conscious of diet trends, margarine companies have altered their products to accommodate the new low-fat/no-fat diets. While this is wonderful for diet shoppers, it is detrimental to cookie production. When I began baking batches of cookies large enough to sell, I converted all the recipes to weight. Now, the new margarine does not contain the same percentage of fat and the cookies are not consistent. I spent several days working with the dough. Some batches contained too much flour; others spread too much. Eventually, after many painstaking attempts, I had a perfect batch of sugar cookies, and my apprehension subsided.

During the redevelopment of my cookie recipes, I made a batch of gingersnaps that did not meet my usual standards. The taste was normal, but the appearance was quite different. I only sell cookies when they look palatable by my standards. I decided that the best use of the misfit cookies was to make a donation. I called Preston Meadow Lutheran Church and asked Betty, the Director of Education, if she could use twelve dozen cookies.

"Sure, we will serve them after services."

Sunday, when we arrived for church, Pastor Anderson said, "Sorry, we are not going to have cookies today." He had taken a bag of them each day to the synod meetings. The council members loved them.

While I was setting the new ingredient portions of my cookies, then I thought of my grandson Sam. At birth, he was born hydrocephalic and had to have a shunt to drain the excess fluid around his brain. He is also on a special high-fiber diet. Even though he eats regularly and enjoys every cookie, as do all my grandchildren, I thought he might like to have a special cookie. I developed a recipe for oatmeal-cranberry cookies. Those had the additional fiber he needed, without the taste of fiber-rich food. Although my cookies often serve medicinal purposes for the soul, this was the first that healed the body. This is the reason I am proud of the Sam Cookie.

Growing and running a business can be a challenge. I often want to contribute to various causes, but it is difficult on my limited budget. How many donations can you make each year? I know that I am unable to make a substantial cash donation, then I thought Wouldn't it be wonderful to be able to donate the cookies for the St. Lucia Fest?

In 1995, I was able to donate all the cookies used for the festival. This event is put on by the Swedish community for an audience of 900 or more. I felt blessed to share the joy of the cookies with so many people.

One customer from Atlanta, Georgia, emailed and asked for the price of the "to-die-for" sugar cookies.

My son-in-law Andrew was quizzing his son Benjamin on what members of the family did as a profession.

"What does Uncle Stu do?"
"He's an air traffic controller and he directs planes."
"What does Grandpa do?"
"He's a builder. He builds houses."
"What does Grandma do?"
"She makes soup and cookies!"

Benjamin called me one morning.

"Grandma, do you think you could come and babysit?"

I said, "In July, Grandma is coming to Minnesota and would be happy to."

"Do you think we could make cookies then?" he asked. "Benjamin," I said, "your Grandma would love to bake cookies with you."

Sometimes I am not sure if he wants me or the cookies.

Once a week, my daughter and I call each other to discuss the past week. I ask her about Sam and Benjamin.

One time, Shelly said that the children were fine and that she and Benjamin had discussed their dreams.

Benjamin had dreamt about the Battle of Jericho. While Benjamin's dream was exciting, Shelly's was equally interesting. Shelly had a dream that she attended a bake-off for sugar cookies. She remembered walking among the tables and hearing the announcer. In her dream, I was the winner. The judges had liked my cookies and were pleased with the texture. The others lost because the bottoms of the cookies were too brown. It is rather amusing that my attribute of perfection towards cookie baking is so thoroughly embedded in the subconscious of my children that it appears in their dreams!

I often refer to The Wooden Spoon as my "cookie ministry." How many times have I poured a cup of coffee, served a cookie, and listened to someone's story?

I have a friend named Rosalie. We have been good friends for decades. I have always admired her, because she is a strong woman and never hesitates to provide strength for those around her. She has suffered many tragedies and handled each one with grace. One day, she and her family had been in my thoughts. I decided to surprise her with some cookies, as she used to love to visit with me over coffee and cookies, so I mailed her three different types of cookies for Valentine's Day. I also knew that she would have plenty for herself and have some left over to share with her grandchildren. I also knew that it was a kind thing to do, but I did not expect to have the effect that I did. Her thank-you note warmed my soul. It read:

"I was having a very down day. The UPS truck drove up and delivered your cookies, and you made my day. I shared them with my friends and family – you were a big hit. I am so lucky and fortunate to have you in my life. What a wonderful feeling inside to be thought about, especially from old friends that I will always be dearest in my heart.

My love and thanks, Rosalie."

The first time I met Emma, she was in her mother's womb. Her mother had been a customer for years and I shared in her anticipation. After Emma was born, we were all delighted. She was such a beautiful baby.

Over time, I saw Emma change from a newborn to a toddler. As she grew, I realized that Emma and I needed a special cookie ritual. Every time her mother brought her into the store, I gave her a cookie. I continued to do this for the next couple of years. Only one cookie. She never asked for a second one or one to take home. She and her mother were quiet people.

One day, for the first time ever, Emma began to cry in the store. The cry gradually became a heavy sob, perplexing her parents and myself. Her parents attempted to comfort her. We were dumbfounded by her constant tears. Nobody could determine the source of her anguish.

Suddenly, the solution occurred to us. Emma had yet to receive her usual cookie. I hurried to the tin, pulled one out and presented it to her. The tears immediately subsided, and she ate it. After that, Emma was herself. From that day forward, without fail, I have remembered Emma's cookie.

The Wooden Spoon is in the oldest house in Plano, Texas. Groups such as the Boy Scouts and Girl Scouts often express interest in touring the grounds.

One afternoon, a troop leader called and asked if her Girl Scout troop could be given a tour. I wanted to accommodate them, so we scheduled one for the next day.

At four o'clock the next day, fifteen young girls came into the shop. We walked through the house, discussing various items and Scandinavian stories. We went through each room, ending in the upstairs. I turned to the girls and said, "I think it is time to teach you to eat a cookie." They all looked to me as if to say, "What do you mean? We have all been doing that for years!" Girl Scouts have been selling cookies for generations. Who was I to teach them about cookies?

I took a tin of Swedish gingersnaps, told them each to take one but not to eat it. They respected my request. Then I taught them the proper way to eat a cookie:

Place the cookie in one hand.
Make a wish.
With your index finger, tap the cookies hard enough to break it.
If it breaks in three pieces, your wish will come true.
If not, just eat and enjoy the cookie.

We were asked to participate in an International Day at the Federal Reserve Bank in Dallas. Jennifer, one of my employees, and I set up a wonderful Scandinavian display. It was beautiful, but we were not attracting any interest. We watched as the crowd ambled around. I asked Jennifer to open a tin of wish cookies. Almost instantly, we were noticed.

We began to teach them to "eat a cookie." Eventually, our booth, which had no attention before, had a line forming. We were excited and amused to teach the proper method of cookie eating. Everyone enjoyed the process.

One afternoon a disheveled little girl came into the shop. "Is it big upstairs?" she asked. I said, "Yes, it is," I said. "If your Mom is willing, she can take you upstairs." (Her mother was shopping next door). Then she asked if I had anything for a quarter.

I said, "No, but I do have something for you." I took the tin of Swedish wish cookies and began explaining them to her. Before I finished, her mother and brother joined us. Now they all knew how to wish with a cookie and to enjoy eating it.

At the Norwegian Society of Texas Christmas party, I had the pleasure of meeting one of God's incredibly special stewards: a lady named Stella Olson. She has done more to teach Norwegian heritage than anyone I have ever met. She taught Norwegian language classes, the art of Norwegian cooking and hosted an annual cookie party.

The cookies were plentiful. She began baking three months prior to the event. She served 100 different treats at the last party she hosted. In early December, she invited her friends and family to enjoy the delicious morsels.

Over the years we became good friends and one day she came into the shop. I poured a cup of coffee and offered her a cookie. Then we sat down to chat. She told me she did not have a location for her party that year and was

rather distressed. I told her that she was more than welcome to hold the gathering upstairs at The Wooden Spoon. After some convincing (she did not want to take advantage of our friendship), she agreed to my suggestion. The party was wonderful, and we celebrated there for several years.

During one of our conversations, she told me that she had never been to Norway. I was saddened by this news. I wanted her to be able to take the trip while she was still physically able but did not have the resources to send her. I brainstormed for days and finally thought of a solution. I took several gifts from the shop, created a raffle, and asked one of my friends, Susie, to be the ticket seller. She agreed because of the reason and did a wonderful job of raising money. I was touched to see the Norwegian community pull together. Countless people came forward with advice and helpful offers. Her friends, Marcie and Ed volunteered to travel with her, making sure she and her luggage arrived at her destination. They sacrificed their personal leisure time to assist her as needed. Another friend, Ann, brought Texas pralines to be used as thank-you gifts for her host family. Dozens of people came forward with "spending money" donations, and SAS Airlines gave us a special price on her ticket. We all wanted this trip to be memorable for her. After all the hard work and planning, we sent Stella Olson, at the age of 85, to Norway. Upon returning, she raved, saying that she had a splendid time.

The next year, her back was severely hurt. Sadly, she announced that she was no longer able to host a cookie party. My response was,

"As long as I have anything to say about it, we will always have a Stella Olson Cookie Party, but you will not do the work."

Now the party is in honor of Stella, a beautiful lady, to thank her for her many years of kindness and dedication to her Norwegian heritage. The Wooden Spoon hosts the party, and each guest brings a tray of cookies to share and enjoy the fellowship begun by one woman who gave so much.

One sunny afternoon, a beautiful and energetic little girl came into the shop with her mother. She was about three years old and full of spunk. Even though I had never seen her before, she boldly came right to me. With the innocence of a child, she said:

"I know your name."

"You do?" I said. "What is it?"

She responded, without hesitation,

"Grandma!"

I said, "Well, if I am Grandma, come and give me a hug."

She happily threw her little arms around my waist and gave a tight squeeze.

I was in awe of her warmth and sincerity. When she let go, I led her to the cookies and shared one with her. She was happy to find both a grandma and a cookie.

A Norwegian family with three boys came to the shop. The middle child was having a particularly trying day. He was a little grumpy and seemed out of sorts. After observing him for a few minutes, I asked him, "Have you got the 'uglies?' You know, I have learned that a cookie can take away the 'uglies.' Would you like one?"

After brief consideration, he decided he would try one. He and his brothers each chose a different kind. unfortunately their first extraction was unsuccessful so they agreed to try again. After one more dose, the "uglies" had vanished and the boys forgot the grief of the day. Thank goodness there were plenty of cookies on hand because going through the day with the "uglies" can become rather, well…ugly.

I gave nine Girl Scouts a tour of the Wooden Spoon and a "trip to Sweden." I started by giving each of them a comic book in Swedish. Then we toured and talked. Many questions and comments were shared. We ended by going upstairs where I served treats and the pepperkaker cookie from Sweden. This gave us time to talk and ask questions. They all thanked me and said goodbye in Swedish. It was such an enjoyable evening!

When my grandson Brandon's cousins Bennie and Russell were about four and six, Susie, their aunt invited us to dinner.

I took a tray of Daim cookies as a hostess gift. Russell was at home, so only Bennie had dinner with us. He and his father were ready to leave but he had a question for me.

"Can I have a cookie to take home for my brother?"

Of course, that was possible. We fixed a tray with several cookies so each boy would have plenty.

I belong to PEO and on several occasions, I have provided my cookies. As with all organizations, they look for new programs. I was asked by the program chairwoman Candace, if I could do a program on my cookies. We decided to title it "For the Love of Cookies."

    As I prepared, I decided it would not be right to just talk about them. I should have a tray to share. Now, what cookie would it be? I wanted to make one they had not experienced before. I decided on the Norwegian Berlin-A-Kranse. It was a fun program, enjoyed by members who were thrilled to have a special cookie. I found it interesting that some asked if they could take one home to their husbands.

One customer wondered how I could make the cookies so perfect. I explained that consistency was the key to future sales. I weigh the ingredients and I weigh each of the cookies. This assures you that consistency is key.

Each December, we offer the Scandinavian holiday drink called Glogg, and pepperkaker cookies. It is fun to hear people reminisce as they sip and eat cookies like grandma used to make.

I have friends who have been confined to their homes for medical or other reasons. If unable to go to their home, I would take two packages of cookies and a pound of Swedish coffee, package it, and include a note, "Enjoy and/or share a cup of coffee and a cookie on me!" Then I mailed them. One friend told me she loved that they were "really cookies".

A young man was in treatment for cancer and our church asked us to provide meals. As I calculated time and energy to make a meal and deliver it to their home, it did not make sense. Instead, I decided to fix a basket filled with snacks, candy, and my cookies, and then send them by UPS. He had an older brother with which to share it. It was well-received.

My best friend Arlene's son was in a serious ATV accident. They live in Minnesota, but my thoughts were with them. There was my best childhood friend who needed help and support. I live far away, so what could I do? I baked a large batch of cookies, taped a gas gift card to it, and mailed it to her. She shared them with those caring for her son.

A mother with her two daughters, Chloe and Morgan, came to buy t-shirts for their Parade of Nations at their school. I asked them what they were doing for it. They were just marching but some would be going in costume. Well, we needed to get them ready to represent Norway. We found a Bunad costume and a Viking costume with a helmet. They were very excited. I made two little gals so happy. They are granddaughters of one of my Bible friends study group.

Good customers came to shop with their three-year-old great-granddaughter. The moment she saw me she said,

"Hi Grandma."

I said, "Hi, come and give me a hug".

She promptly did.

Then she said, "Grandma, could I have some chocolate candy?"

I am sure you guessed the answer! After the chocolate candy, we shared a cookie.

My brother-in-law is a retired teacher. If you make him anything, he grades you. Of course, you never get better than an A-minus because there is always room for improvement. My sister had surgery and was unable to bake his favorite cookies, so I thought it would be nice to send him a batch of oatmeal raisin-nut. She had told me he liked them with a lot of nuts, so I got busy and made him a batch.

He called to thank me. However, I was anxious to know my grade. He said I got an A-plus. Incredible!

I was visiting my son and family and we were discussing food, meals, and recipes. Nick, my grandson was about seven or eight years old when he said to me, "Grandma, do you have my recipe for brownies?" I was amazed, but his father told me he bakes rather often. That was not surprising because my son Stu is a great cook. This is the recipe he gave me. Yes, they are delicious.

NICK'S BROWNIES

Mix well:
2 cups sugar
1 cup butter

Add:
4 eggs well beaten
2 teaspoons vanilla
¼ teaspoon salt
¾ cup cocoa

Mix well then add:
1¼ cups flour
1 teaspoon baking powder

Stir in ½ cup chopped nuts. Bake in 9 x 11-inch pan in 350° oven for 30-35 minutes. Cool. Cut into squares.

Recipe Notes

For many years my church, Salem Lutheran held three smorgasbords each summer to raise funds to sustain itself. The favorite part of the meal was the treats the bakers made. I would like to share a few of the recipes with you and give credit to a few of the bakers who worked so hard and baked thousands of treats over the years.

Salem Lutheran Church, Longville, Minn.

Recipe Notes

DOROTHEA'S RECIPE FOR SALTED PEANUT COOKIES

Cream together:
1 cup shortening
¾ cup white sugar
¾ cup brown sugar

Add:
1 egg beaten well
1 teaspoon vanilla

Add:
2 cups flour
1 teaspoon baking powder
1 teaspoon soda

Mix well then add:
1 cup cornflakes
1 cup raw oatmeal
1 cup salted peanuts

Form into balls the size of a walnut. Dip in granulated sugar. Bake at 350° for about 8-10 minutes.

Recipe Notes

INEZ'S RECIPE FOR LEMON BARS

Mix like pie crust:
1 cup flour
½ cup butter
¼ teaspoon salt
Press into the bottom of an 8 X 8-inch pan.
Bake at 350° for 15-20 minutes or until lightly browned.

Beat together:
2 eggs
3 tablespoons lemon juice and zest from one lemon
2½ tablespoons flour
½ teaspoon baking powder
1 cup sugar
Beat well. Pour over baked crust.
Bake at 350° for about 25 minutes.

Frost and drizzle with:
1½ cups powdered sugar
2 tablespoons lemon juice

When cool, cut into squares.

Recipe Notes

MARILYN'S RECIPE FOR FRUITCAKE COOKIES

Mix well:
1 cup butter
1½ cups brown sugar

Add:
2 eggs beaten
Mix well then add:
2½ cups flour
1 teaspoon cinnamon
1 teaspoon vanilla
1 teaspoon salt
1 teaspoon soda

Add:
1 package candied pineapple chunks
1 pound candied cherries
1 pound dates, diced
1 cup each filberts, pecans, and walnuts

Mix well. Drop by teaspoonfuls on cookie sheets. Bake at 350° for 8-10 minutes or until slightly brown.

Recipe Notes

LOLA'S RECIPE FOR CHEESECAKE BARS

Mix:

⅓ cup brown sugar
1 cup flour
½ cup melted butter
½ cup walnuts or pecans

Press ¾ mixture into the bottom of an 8 x 8-inch pan that you have sprayed with baking oil. Reserve the rest to sprinkle over the filling.

Filling. Mix well:

8 ounces cream cheese
¼ cup white sugar
1 egg
1 teaspoon vanilla
1 tablespoon lemon juice
2 tablespoons heavy cream

Pour over crust. Top with reserved crumbs. Bake at 350° for 25 minutes. When cool, cut into squares.

Recipe Notes

MARILYN'S RECIPE FOR AUNT SALLY COOKIES

Mix well:
1 cup Crisco
1½ cups white sugar

Add:
1 cup molasses
½ cup hot coffee

Mix well and add:
1 teaspoon ginger
½ teaspoon nutmeg
¼ teaspoon cloves
¼ teaspoon salt

Mix and add:
5 cups flour
2 teaspoons soda

Mix well and refrigerate overnight:
Roll out on pastry cloth to about ⅛-¼ inch thick. Use oval or rectangular cookie cutter. Place on cookie sheets and bake at 350° for 10-12 minutes. When cool, make icing. Frost each on the bottom of the cookie. Please use speed as the icing will set very fast.

Icing, In saucepan put:
1 envelope Knox unflavored gelatin
1 cup white sugar
1 cup cold water
Bring to a rolling boil. Simmer for 10 minutes. Cool.
Pour into mixer bowl.

Add:
1 ¾ cups powdered sugar
¾ teaspoon baking soda
1 teaspoon vanilla

Beat until firm and spreadable. Frost each cookie on the bottom.

Recipe Notes

DOROTHEA'S RECIPE FOR DATE BARS

Cream:
1 cup shortening
1 cup brown sugar

Add:
1 egg

Mix in:
1¾ cup oatmeal
1¾ cup flour
1 teaspoon soda
½ teaspoon salt

Put ½ of this mixture into the bottom of an 8 x 11 pan. Reserve the rest to put on the top after the filling.

Filling:
In saucepan combine
1 pound dates, snipped
½ cup sugar
½ cup orange juice

Slowly bring to a boil and simmer until well mixed and thickened. Pour over the mixture in the pan. Top with reserved mixture. Bake at 350° for 30-35 minutes.

Recipe Notes

WANITA'S RECIPE FOR CHERRY NUT BARS

Mix like pie crust:
2 cups flour
1 cup margarine
½ cup brown sugar
Press evenly onto a cookie sheet. Bake 15 minutes.

Meanwhile mix:
2 eggs and one yolk
1½ cups brown sugar
¼ cup flour
1 teaspoon salt
½ cup chopped maraschino cherries (drain before chopping)
½ cup nuts (your choice, walnuts or pecans are best)

Pour over crust. Bake 20 min.

When cool frost with:
2 cups powdered sugar
2 tablespoons melted butter
Enough cherry juice to make it spreadable.

Cut in small bars and enjoy!

Recipe Notes

PUMPKIN CHEESECAKE

Raised in a large family, my mother taught us how to be frugal and not to waste anything. Taking her advice, I came up with a delicious pumpkin cheesecake recipe using the broken gingersnaps. At the Wooden Spoon, we invite you to have a cookie or two while you shop or, we will teach you how to eat a cookie. The "Swedish Wish Cookie." Often, we end up with broken ones so instead of throwing them out, we use them to make the crust for this cheesecake. Crush one box of Anna ginger thins for crumbs. You may want to use a blender.

Add:
¼ cup melted butter
Press into an 8″ or 10″ springform pan
Refrigerate while you make the cheesecake.

Blend as you add the following ingredients into a large mixing bowl:
2 8-ounce packages cream cheese
1 pint cultured sour cream
1 cup heavy whipping cream
1¾ cups sugar
1 can pumpkin
4 eggs
2 teaspoons cinnamon
½ teaspoon cloves
2 tablespoons lemon juice
2 tablespoons flour

Mix on high speed for 2 minutes. Pour into springform pan. Bake at 350° for 20 minutes. Then bake at 300° for 40 minutes. Turn off oven and leave cheesecake in oven for one hour. Refrigerate. Serve with a dollop of whipped cream, then dust with cinnamon.

The modern world is much more confusing and hurried than it once was. People rush through the day, barely slowing down to visit with friends or simply relax. Cookies are not complicated. They are sweet, simple, and rarely a disappointment. People enjoy cookies in times of grief or celebration. Without fail, they are a loyal treat.

As each person travels down the road of life, it is necessary to remember and share these qualities of simplicity, sweetness, and reliability. Through these actions, everybody will have individual cookie stories to share, so sprinkle cookie crumbs in new and old places and enjoy life's simple pleasures.

A cookie and a smile go a long way!

HERMITS

Blend:
1½ cups white sugar
½ cup butter

Add:
2 eggs
1 teaspoon soda dissolved in 5 tablespoons sweet milk
1 teaspoon cinnamon
½ teaspoon cloves
¾ teaspoon nutmeg

Mix well.

Add:
2 cups flour
2 cups ground raisins

Add flour until dough is stiff enough to roll. Cut diamond shapes with a cookie wheel. Bake flat on ungreased cookie sheet at 350° oven for 6-9 minutes or until slightly brown.

Recipe Notes

SOUR CREAM COOKIES

Blend:
1 cup buttery Crisco®
1½ cups sugar

Add:
1 cup soured cream (not commercial)
1 teaspoon soda
¼ teaspoon salt
1½ teaspoons almond or white vanilla
2 cups flour (You will need extra flour to roll out cookies)

Mix well. Roll very thinly on pastry board. Cut in your favorite shapes with cookie cutters. Decorate with colored sugars or bake plain to be iced later. Place on ungreased cookie sheet. Bake at 325° for 5-7 minutes or until slightly browned.

Recipe Notes

BERLIN-A-KRANSE

Hard boil 3 eggs. Peel and cool. Remove and mash egg yolks very finely with a fork or press through a sieve.

Blend together:
1 pound butter
½ pound white sugar

Add:
sieved egg yolks
4 raw egg yolks (save whites)
1½ teaspoons almond extract
Mix well.

Add:
1½ pounds flour
Mix well. The dough will be soft and pliable. Using a shallow bowl, beat egg whites until foamy. Take a teaspoon of the dough, roll into a rope, then twist into a figure eight. Dip into beaten egg whites, then into pearl sugar. Place on ungreased baking sheet. Bake at 325° for 8-10 minutes.

Recipe Notes

FATTIGMANN

In medium-sized, bowl put:
2 whole eggs
2 yolks
Beat until foamy.

Add:
4 tablespoons white sugar
4 tablespoons whipping cream
2 tablespoons melted butter
1 teaspoon vanilla or ½ teaspoon cardamom

Add:
2 cups flour

Prepare deep fat fryer. Bring to 350°-370°.

Place about ½ cup of the dough onto a floured pastry cloth. Roll very thin. Cut into diamond shapes with a pastry wheel. Drop into a hot fryer. When nicely browned, remove from the heat, drain on a paper towel and sprinkle with white sugar. Continue until all dough is used.

Recipe Notes

KRUMKAKER

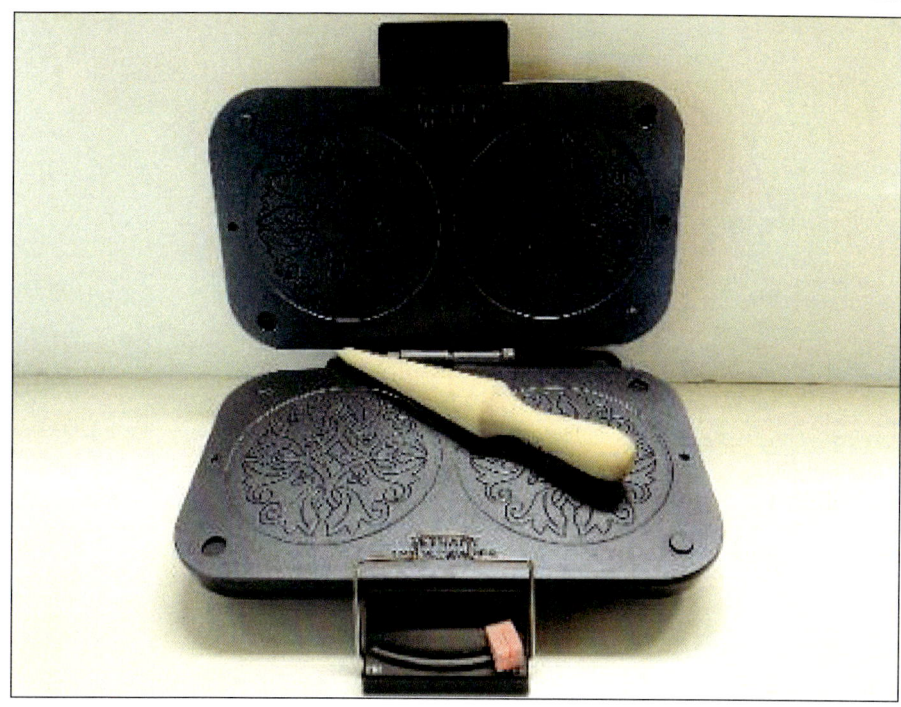

(You will need a Krumkaker iron to make these.)

Beat until fluffy and yellow-colored 3 whole eggs

Add:
½ cup melted butter
1 cup white sugar
1 teaspoon flavoring, (lemon, almond, vanilla, or cardamom)
1 cup heavy whipping cream
1½ cups flour

Mix well.

Heat krumkaker iron. Follow directions on your iron for heating. It will make a difference if you are using an electric or non-electric iron.

Put a teaspoon of batter on iron. Bake until slightly browned. Remove from iron and wrap around a wooden cone. Cool. Remove from cone. Continue this process until all batter is used. Store in airtight container. These may be eaten plain or filled with whipped cream and fruit.

Note: Fill just before serving to avoid becoming soft.

Recipe Notes

SANDBAKKELS

You will need Sandbakkel tins for these.

Mix:
½ cup butter
½ cup Crisco®
1 cup white sugar

Add:
1 egg
½ teaspoon almond extract
1½ cups flour
¼ teaspoon baking powder

Blend well.

Press dough into sandbakkel tins. Make sure dough is spread evenly. Place tins on cookie sheets. Bake in 325° oven for 15 minutes or until slightly browned. Let tins cool. Invert and gently tap the bottom to release cookies. Cool completely. Store in airtight a container.

Recipe Notes

ICE BOX COOKIES

Mix:
¾ cup white sugar
¾ cup brown sugar
1 cup buttery Crisco®

Add:
4 tablespoons whipping cream
2 teaspoons vanilla
Mix well.

Add:
2 cups flour
2 teaspoons baking soda

When dough is well blended, add ½ cup walnuts, pecans, or toffee chips. Form into rolls, wrap in Saran® wrap and place in refrigerator for several hours or overnight. This dough can also be frozen. Cut each roll into ¼ inch slices. Place on ungreased baking sheet. Bake at 350° for 10-12 minutes.

Recipe Notes

COCONUT-CHERRY MACAROONS

Beat 2 egg whites until stiff and dry.

In separate bowl, mix well:
⅔ cup sweetened condensed milk
½ teaspoon salt
1½ teaspoons almond flavoring

Add:
2½ cups coconut
½ cup chopped maraschino cherries

Carefully fold in the egg whites.

Take a tablespoon full of dough and drop onto well-oiled baking pan. Bake at 325° for about 15 minutes.

Recipe Notes

OATMEAL RAISIN FILLED COOKIES

Blend together:
1¼ cup brown sugar
1 cup buttery Crisco®

Add:
1 egg
1 teaspoon vanilla
½ teaspoon cinnamon
2 teaspoons baking soda
2½ cups oatmeal
2 cups flour

Mix well. Roll out and cut with cookie cutter. Bake at 350° for 8-10 minutes.

Raisin Filling
¾ cup white sugar
1 cup ground raisins
½ cup orange juice
1 tablespoon flour

Slowly bring it to a boil. Cook until thick and stir often. Cool. Store in covered dish in refrigerator. Just before serving, top one cookie with raisin filling and top with second cookie, (sandwich style). Best with a cold glass of milk or a steamy cup of coffee.

Recipe Notes

PEANUT BUTTER COOKIES

Mix well:
¾ cup white sugar
¾ cup brown sugar
1 cup buttery Crisco®
1 cup peanut butter

Add:
2 eggs
1½ teaspoons vanilla
1 teaspoon baking soda
3 cups flour
Mix well.

Take a tablespoon full of dough, roll into a ball, place on ungreased cookie sheet. Flatten with a fork that you have dipped in flour. Bake at 350° for 10-12 minutes.

Recipe Notes

SPRITZ

Mix well:
½ cup sugar
¾ cup butter

Add and mix well:
1 egg yolk
1 teaspoon almond extract

Add:
2 cups flour
¼ teaspoon salt
Mix well.

Fill cookie press to make the shapes you desire. Decorate as you wish. You can color the dough with a few drops of food coloring for a fun effect. Fill cookie press with dough. Press dough through press unto ungreased cookie sheet. Bake at 325° for 8-10 minutes. For variety, tint dough before putting in press.

Recipe Notes

SPICE COOKIES

Mix well:
1 cup buttery Crisco®
2 cups brown sugar

Add:
2 eggs
½ cup buttermilk
1 teaspoon soda
1 teaspoon baking powder
½ teaspoon salt
2 teaspoons cinnamon
1 teaspoon nutmeg
½ teaspoon cloves
Mix well.

Add:
2 cups flour
1 chopped nuts
1 cup chopped dates
1 cup ground raisins

Drop by teaspoons unto ungreased cookie sheet. Bake at 350° for 10-12 minutes. Store in covered container.

Recipe Notes

GINGERSNAP/PEPPERKAKER

Mix well:
1½ cups buttery Crisco®
2 cups white sugar

Add:
¼ cup molasses
2 eggs
½ teaspoon salt
1½ teaspoons cinnamon
¾ teaspoon cloves
¾ teaspoon ginger
2 teaspoons baking soda
4 cups flour
Mix well.

Take a tablespoon of dough, roll into a ball, dip in white sugar and place on ungreased cookie sheet. Bake at 350° for 10-12 minutes.

Recipe Notes

SUGAR COOKIES

Mix well:
2 cups buttery Crisco®
2 cups white sugar

Add:
2 eggs
½ teaspoon salt
1 teaspoon white vanilla
1 teaspoon almond flavoring
1 teaspoon baking soda
1 teaspoon cream of tartar
4 cups flour
Mix well.

Take one tablespoon of dough, roll in a ball, dip in white sugar and place on ungreased cookie sheet. Bake 10-12 minutes at 350°. Serve cookies plain or frosted.

To make my signature Lemon-Iced Cookies:
2 cups powdered sugar
1 tablespoon Crisco® oil
2 drops yellow food coloring
Mix with lemon juice to the consistency you want. Frost cookies and enjoy.

Recipe Notes

CHOCOLATE CHIP-DAIM/HEATH COOKIES

Mix well:
3/4 cup white sugar
3/4 cup brown sugar
1 cup buttery Crisco®

Add:
2 eggs
1 1/2 teaspoons vanilla
1 teaspoon caramel flavoring
1 teaspoon baking soda
3 cups flour

Add one cup crushed Daim pieces and one package semi sweet chocolate chips. Mix well.

Drop by teaspoonfuls on ungreased cookie sheet. Bake 10-12 minutes.

Recipe Notes

CHOCOLATE PECAN COOKIES

Melt and cool:
3 oz. unsweetened chocolate

Mix:
¾ cup Crisco®
¾ cup butter
2 cups sugar

Add:
Melted chocolate
½ cup cocoa

Mix well, then add:
3 cups flour
2 teaspoons very finely crushed carbonate of ammonia
1 teaspoon vanilla
Mix well.

Take tablespoons of dough. Roll into 1˝ ball. Press pecan half on top. Place on ungreased cookie sheet. Bake at 300° for 12-15 minutes.

Recipe Notes

DAIM COOKIES

Mix well:
¾ cup white sugar
¾ cup brown sugar
1 cup buttery Crisco®

Add:
4 tablespoons whipping cream
1 teaspoon vanilla
1 teaspoon caramel flavoring
Mix well.

Add:
2 cups flour
2 teaspoons baking soda
1 cup crushed Daim candy pieces

Roll dough into small balls. Bake at 350° for 10-12 minutes When they come out of the oven, quickly put a chocolate kiss on the center of each.
Note: Be sure to have your kisses unwrapped before you start baking these.

Take tablespoons of dough. Roll into 1˝ ball. Press pecan half on top. Place on ungreased ʻ sheet. Bake at 300° for 12-15 minutes.

Recipe Notes

SAMMY'S OATMEAL-CRANBERRY COOKIES

In a large bowl mix together:
¾ cup white sugar
¾ cup brown sugar
1 cup buttery Crisco®

Add:
2 eggs
1½ teaspoons vanilla
¾ teaspoon cinnamon
¾ teaspoon salt
1½ teaspoons soda

Add:
1½ cups oatmeal
2 cups flour
1½ cups dried cranberries

Mix well. Form to walnut size balls. Place on ungreased cookie sheet. Flatten slightly. Bake at 350° for 10-12 minutes.

Note: Raisins, pecans, walnuts, dates, or currants can be substituted for the dried cranberries for an array of cookies or split the dough in two and add different fruits or nuts to each half.

ABOUT THE AUTHORS

Gwen Workman

I was born and raised in rural Minnesota. In 1959, I married Jim Workman. Together we owned a motel and a restaurant. We were blessed with three children and five grandsons. I have always been involved in my church and community and I love to bring people together. What a better way to do that with the help of cookies. Today, I live in Texas where I own the Wooden Spoon Scandinavian Shop and Cultural Center. Stop in and enjoy a cup of coffee and a cookie and share life's greatest pleasures.

Virginia Jonas

Virginia is the second of five daughters born to parents of Finnish and Danish descent. She is an attorney in Indianapolis where she lives with her husband, Kevin, and their two children, Zachary and Madelyn. Virginia worked for me for several years, and during that time we formed a beautiful friendship. Together, we wrote *A Cooky Journal*. *My Cooky Journal* uses the original but has been updated with new stories, pictures, and recipes.

Order Additional Copies of A Cooky Journal
The Wooden Spoon
1617 Avenue K, Plano, TX 75074